# VIP
## VERY IMPORTANT PEOPLE

# DR. MAE JEMISON

Brave Rocketeer

HEATHER ALEXANDER

INTERIOR ILLUSTRATIONS BY
JEN BRICKING

**HARPER**
*An Imprint of HarperCollinsPublishers*

VIP: Dr. Mae Jemison

Copyright © 2021 by HarperCollins Publishers

Interior illustrations copyright © 2021 by HarperCollins Publishers

www.harpercollinschildrens.com

Library of Congress Control Number: 2020938938

ISBN 978-0-06-288970-6 (pbk.) — ISBN 978-0-06-297808-0

Illustrations by Jen Bricking

Typography by Torborg Davern

20 21 22 23 24   PC/LSCC   10 9 8 7 6 5 4 3 2 1

❖

First Edition

*To all kids who dream of the stars and beyond*

# Contents

**Prologue**       1

**Chapter 1:** When I Grow Up       6

**Chapter 2:** Finding Courage       23

**Chapter 3:** Letting the Wind Blow       38

**Chapter 4:** Doctor Time       46

**Chapter 5:** Getting In       59

**Chapter 6:** Facing Her Fears       69

**Chapter 7:** Lift-off!       82

**Chapter 8:** Busy in Space       91

**Chapter 9:** Next Chapters       99

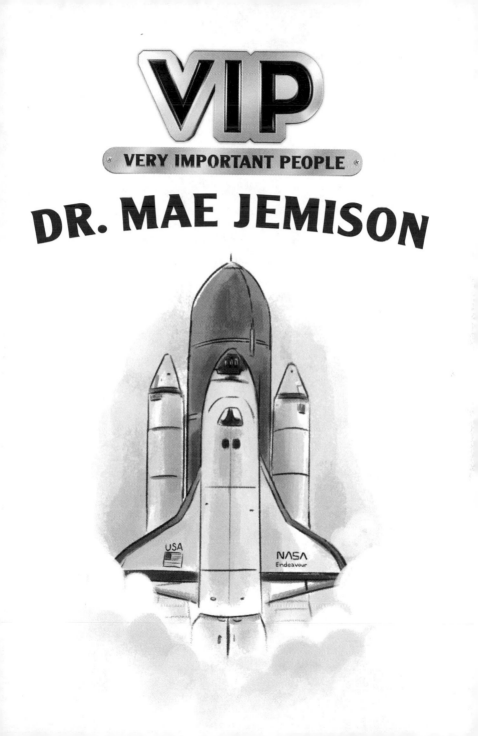

# Prologue

Mae Jemison held her breath as the lunar module touched the surface of the moon. She stared at the grainy image on her family's television. Her brown eyes grew wide watching American astronauts Neil Armstrong and Buzz Aldrin step out. They would be the first humans to walk on the moon.

"Wow! The moon!" cried twelve-year-old Mae.

It was July 21, 1969. Along with hundreds of millions of people all over the world, Mae was witnessing the historic Apollo 11 mission to the moon. She'd been waiting for this special day for a long time.

Mae had been obsessed with the space program

since she was six years old. She knew *a lot* about space, the stars, and how rockets flew. She knew when each mission would take place and what it was supposed to accomplish. She'd read books that gave step-by-step details of how a human would go to the moon.

*What if I were way up there?* she wondered.

Mae closed her eyes and imagined herself

floating through space. She wore an astronaut suit. She walked on the moon. She made important scientific discoveries.

When she opened her eyes, she saw photos flash onto the television screen of the American astronauts who'd gone to space and ones who were training to go. She stared at their faces. They looked nothing like her.

They were all men.

They were all white.

*Where are the women?* wondered Mae. *Where are the people of color?*

"What will the aliens think?" she asked her family. "Will they think that Earth is just made up of white men?"

Her parents explained it was the way things were. The way things had always been.

Mae thought it was "stupid" that only white men got to go into space. A huge solar system filled with stars, planets, and who knew what else waited out there. She wanted so badly to explore it. Why did she have to be left out?

*The moon is only the first step,* Mae thought. *When I grow up, people will fly to space as easily as they fly across the country in airplanes.*

Somehow.

Someday.

Mae planned to fly to the stars, too.

## CHAPTER 1

# When I Grow Up

Mae Carol Jemison was born on October 17, 1956, in Decatur, Alabama. The nurses at the hospital gathered around her. *What an incredibly happy baby!* they all cried. Little Mae was full of energy.

Mae was the third child of Dorothy and Charlie Jemison. She had an older brother, Ricky, and an older sister, Ada Sue. Her father was a roofer and a carpenter, and her mother would later become an elementary school teacher.

Both her parents had spent their whole lives in Alabama, but they decided to leave when Mae was three years old. Mae's mother had dropped out of college to care for her sick parents. Back then in

Alabama, most Black women could only find work cleaning the houses of white people. Dorothy Jemison knew she was meant to do much more. So Mae's family moved to Chicago, Illinois.

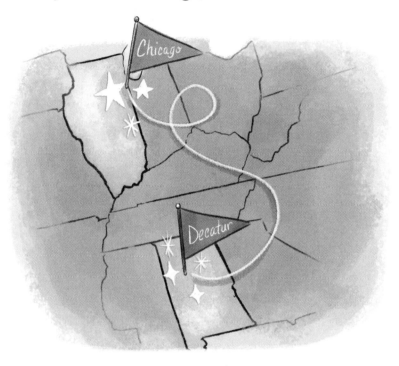

In Chicago, Mae's mom graduated from college and became a teacher. She even went on to get her master's degree. Dorothy taught her children that with hard work they could achieve anything.

# 10 Things Women Couldn't Do in the 1960s and 1970s

When Mae was growing up, women in America didn't have a lot of the legal rights or opportunities they have today. Many didn't have jobs or only worked in careers that were thought to be suited to women— nurse, teacher, sales clerk, or secretary. They were often treated as second-class citizens compared with men. In the 1960s and 1970s, women started to protest this unequal treatment. They marched and wrote articles championing women's rights. Laws and society began to change.

Did you know that when Mae was a girl, women couldn't . . .

1. **Get a credit card:** A bank could refuse to issue a credit card to an unmarried woman, and if she was married, her husband's signature was needed. The Equal Credit Opportunity Act of 1974 made it illegal to refuse a credit card to a woman based on her gender.

2. **Serve on a jury:** Although every state's law was different (Utah allowed women to sit on a jury in 1879), most states wouldn't let women on a jury. Women were thought to be needed in the home. They were said to be too delicate to hear about gory crimes and too sympathetic to make objective decisions. In 1973, women were finally allowed to be jurors in all fifty states.

3.  **Attend some Ivy League universities:** Yale and Princeton didn't accept female students until 1969. Columbia didn't until 1983.

4.  **Attend a military academy:** The United States Military Academy at West Point first admitted women cadets in 1976.

5.  **Serve in combat:** Women were not allowed on the front lines for ground combat until 2015.

6.  **Practice law:** In the 1960s, 90 percent of all law firms refused to hire a woman lawyer.

7.  **Keep their jobs while pregnant:** Until 1978, women could be fired from their jobs for being pregnant.

8. **Earn equal money as men:** In 1963, women earned only fifty-nine cents for every dollar a man earned. (In 2018, women earned approximately eighty cents for every dollar a man earned. African American and Latina women earned less.)

9. **Run the Boston Marathon:** Women were not officially allowed to race until 1972.

10. **Become a NASA astronaut:** Women were not accepted into the training program until 1978.

Mae started kindergarten at her neighborhood school on the South Side of Chicago. She was a bright, curious child who could already read and count. One day the teacher asked the class, "What do you want to be when you grow up?"

Mae's little hand shot into the air. But the teacher called on the other five- and six-year-olds first. "Police officer," "teacher," "mother," they replied one after the other. Finally the teacher came to Mae.

"I want to be a scientist," Mae declared.

The teacher stared in confusion at Mae. "Don't you mean a nurse?"

In 1961, most people thought you had to be a white man to be a scientist. Women were believed to be less intelligent, especially in science and math. African Americans weren't given the chance to study advanced science at college or given scientific jobs, just because of the color of their skin. Mae was a girl *and* African American, so her teacher thought it was impossible she'd ever be a scientist.

Mae didn't think it was impossible. Not at all.

She put her hands on her hips and said, "No, I mean a scientist." Mae loved science. There were so many marvelous things to learn about! Pus was one of them. Mae once got a splinter in her thumb. It became infected, and yellow pus oozed out. She asked her mother about it, and her mother told her to look up "pus" in the library. Mae learned that pus fights infection and helps bodies heal. How amazing that her body could do that!

Mae spent hours and hours in the library. She read books on dinosaurs and evolution. She read about biology, the study of life, and about astronomy, the study of outer space. She learned the different con-stellations and the names of stars in the galaxy.

Mae was fascinated by the stars. She didn't have a telescope, so she'd visit Chicago's Adler Planetarium to see the night sky better. It amazed her that the stars she saw now had been there in the age of the dinosaurs. Stars were timeless, and by look-ing at them, Mae felt connected to everything and everyone. It was a powerful feeling.

# Answers to Some Big Questions Mae Wondered About

**How many stars are in the universe?**

No one knows exactly how many stars there are in the universe, but scientists estimate there are over two hundred billion stars just in our galaxy. Did you know there are more stars in the universe than grains of sand on Earth?

**What was the universe like in the beginning?**

Our universe is almost fourteen billion years old. Scientists think the universe started in a massive explosion known as the big bang. The universe began as a tiny dot and quickly grew bigger and bigger. It's still expanding today.

**How big is "outer space"?**

No one knows the answer to this mind-boggling question, especially since many scientists believe outer space doesn't have a boundary or an end. However, scientists estimate there are two trillion galaxies in the visible universe.

**What big questions do you wonder about?**

In the summertime, Mae would often go fishing with her uncle Louis. He explained that stars were really little suns, and they looked so small because they were so many miles away. The more she stared up at the stars, the more curious Mae became. She began to wonder: *How many stars are in the universe? What was the universe like in the beginning? How big is outer space?* She returned to the library day after day to search for answers and learn more about science.

One day in the library, she accidentally picked up a science-fiction book instead of a nonfiction book. She began to read. Quickly she became a sci-fi fan. "In science fiction, I saw the hope that humans would do better, that we would advance," she wrote later in her autobiography. But it made her angry that women weren't ever the scientists or the heroes in these books. Then she discovered her first sci-fi female hero in *A Wrinkle in Time*, by Madeleine L'Engle. Mac read this book over and over again.

At age ten, Mae first announced that she wanted to go to space. Her parents told her that NASA— the National Aeronautics and Space Administration—

didn't allow women to be astronauts.

"That's the dumbest thing in the world," said Mae. She argued that everyone looks up at the stars and wonders about them, so everyone deserves a chance to go to space.

Her parents agreed. However, they weren't sure if NASA would ever let a girl become an astronaut. They also explained that, because of racism, being Black meant she'd have to be twice as talented as a white person to get anywhere. And being a Black woman? Well, that would make achieving her dreams even harder still.

But her parents encouraged her to try and dream big. They believed Mae could break boundaries—and their belief gave her confidence.

Around that same time, *Star Trek* came on television. It was an action-adventure show about all different kinds of people working together on a spaceship. *Star Trek* featured characters such as Lieutenant Uhura (an African American woman), Lieutenant Sulu (a Japanese man), and Mr. Spock (an alien!). Mae's imagination soared.

*Lieutenant Uhura looks like me,* thought Mae.

Mae couldn't find a real-life role model, so Lieutenant Uhura became her role model. Suddenly, her dream of going to space seemed reasonable. If a Black woman could work in space on TV, surely someday it would happen in the real world.

## CHAPTER 2

# Finding Courage

Around the dinner table, Mae's parents often told stories of people such as Daniel Hale Williams, a Black doctor who performed the first successful heart surgery, and Elijah McCoy, a Black inventor who made trains run better. They showed Mae that African Americans had a long history of being inventors, athletes, businesspeople, and doctors. They taught Mae to be proud of being Black.

When Mae was eight years old, she, her mother, and her sister decided to celebrate their African beauty by cutting their hair really short and leaving it natural. Mae didn't care that people mistook her for a boy or that she was the only girl in her class with short hair. She liked the powerful message it sent to her friends.

In the 1960s, while Mae was growing up, many people were participating in the civil rights movement. Even though the United States was founded on the promise that "all men are created equal," since the beginning, African Americans have experienced racism and discrimination. The civil rights movement actively fought for America to hold true to its promise. Protests were held around the country.

One of the most respected and famous civil rights protesters was Dr. Martin Luther King Jr. He gave powerful speeches about equality and justice for all, regardless of skin color. Mae was inspired by his message and his bravery. She was proud that he struggled to change beliefs that were wrong and ignorant.

# Important Civil Rights Protests

Even though slavery was officially declared illegal after the Civil War, many Southern states refused to grant African Americans the same civil rights as whites. African Americans were segregated (separated). They were forced to go to different schools, to sit in the back of buses, and to use separate restrooms, and they were not allowed to vote. In the 1950s and 1960s, people used protests to challenge racial segregation. Some of the most significant protests were:

## Montgomery Bus Boycott

In 1955, an African American woman named Rosa Parks was arrested because she wouldn't give up her seat on the bus to a white male passenger. This led Dr. Martin

Luther King Jr. to start the Montgomery bus boycott. For over a year, African Americans stopped using public transportation to protest unfair treatment.

## March on Washington

In 1963, more than two hundred thousand people gathered on the Mall in Washington, DC, to show the government they were upset and angry about the discrimination of

African Americans. Dr. King gave his famous "I Have a Dream" speech on the steps of the Lincoln Memorial. This march helped pass the Civil Rights Act of 1964, which made segregation in public places and in the workplace against the law.

### "Bloody Sunday" March from Selma

On March 7, 1965, about six hundred protesters tried to march from Selma, Alabama, to

the state capital in Montgomery to call attention to the lack of voting rights for African Americans. The police used violence to stop them. The attack on the peaceful marchers was filmed and shown on the news, attracting national support for the cause.

## Chicago Freedom Movement

In 1966, Dr. King led marches in Chicago to protest segregated housing. People threw things at the marchers, and Dr. King was hit in the head with a rock. These marches helped bring about the 1968 Fair Housing Act.

Dr. Martin Luther King Jr. was shot and killed by a white gunman when Mae was eleven years old. His assassination angered many African Americans, and right after his death, riots broke out close to her home in Chicago. People were frustrated by racial inequality. Nearby stores were broken into and looted. People were killed. Chicago's mayor sent the National Guard to patrol the city and ordered them to use force to control the riots. Mae peeked out her back screen door as soldiers, dressed in camouflage uniforms and holding rifles, marched single-file

down her empty street. What would happen if they saw her, a young Black girl? Would they shoot her?

Her body trembled in terror. But being that scared also made her angry.

This was her country, too. She hadn't done anything wrong. She was good at school and good at home. So why was she hiding and trembling?

"I reminded myself that I was as much a part of this United States as the guardsmen," she remembers. Then and there, Mae promised herself she'd never let anyone or anything make her that frightened again.

That promise helped Mae a year later.

Mae had skipped seventh grade because she was so smart, so she was only twelve years old when she started high school. Even though she was tall for her age, Mae was scared walking through the crowded high school halls. She refused to let it show. Of course, it helped to have an older brother and sister at the school. Ricky and Ada Sue made sure no one teased her.

Mae liked trying new activities. She even auditioned for the school musical, *West Side Story.* She dreamed of playing Maria, the star role. She practiced Maria's songs and dance over and over. Did she get the part? No. Mae was *horrible* at singing. She was completely off-key!

However, Mae was great at dancing. Throughout her life, she took modern, jazz, ballet, and African dance lessons. She hoped to someday have a room at home where she could pirouette, plié, jump, and sweat. What did Mae love more—dance or science? She couldn't decide.

When she was a junior in high school, Mae wanted to find an original topic for her science-fair project. "You're always talking about space exploration," said her mom. "Why don't you think about something else?" She suggested sickle cell anemia.

"What's that?" Mae asked.

But her mom wouldn't tell her. She liked to throw out new ideas or new words and challenge Mae to learn about them herself.

Mae was always up for the challenge.

First Mae went to the library. She discovered that sickle cell anemia was an inherited blood disease found mostly in people with African ancestry. What next? She needed to know more about blood. Should she call the local hospital? What if they hung up on her? Or treated her like a little kid?

*Maybe I should just do an outer space project,* thought Mae. *That would be easier.*

But Mae finally gathered her courage. She called and asked to speak to the hematology lab technician. Hematology is the study of blood. The lab technician was nice. He invited her to come down to the hospital.

*Now?* Mae panicked. She'd never taken the bus and the train alone across Chicago. What if she got lost? Maybe she shouldn't go.

Once again, Mae gathered her courage and she found her way there. The technician was an older African American man. He answered Mae's questions. He was so impressed with her that he asked her to help out in the lab.

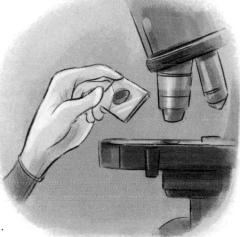

Mae went into the lab twice a week.

She was also able to work on her science-fair project there, mixing solutions and testing blood samples. One day, a white doctor in a white lab coat noticed her. He was in charge of the hematology department. She timidly told him about her project.

"What is your hypothesis?" he asked.

Mae, who'd always been confident talking about science, didn't know what to say. She didn't have one. He reminded her that to do a science project properly, she first had to do more research and come

up with a hypothesis. A hypothesis is a prediction that can be tested—kind of like an educated guess. Mae wondered if she was too inexperienced to be doing a project like this.

But Mae didn't give up. She went back to the library. She returned to the lab with a good hypothesis. The doctor thought she was very smart. From then on, he made time in his busy schedule and taught her how to properly do experiments. Mae realized that if she'd let her fear stop her from making the phone call, getting on the bus, or talking to the doctor, she would have missed this important lab experience.

What about her science-fair project? Mae's project won first place at her school competition—and then it won first place in the citywide high school competition! She had worked hard and was proud of herself.

## CHAPTER 3

# Letting the Wind Blow

Mae waited nervously with her parents in the busy Chicago airport. She was only sixteen years old, but she was already headed to Stanford University in California. Her stomach twisted. Mae had never

been so far away from her family. She'd never been to California. *What would college be like?*

Mae loved it! She met kids from all over the country. They thought it was cool that she was the youngest in their dorm. A friend nicknamed her "Smiley" because she smiled so much that first month.

One of the first classes she took freshman year was general chemistry. Always eager, Mae found a seat in the front row of the lecture hall. She raised her hand all the time. But the professor never called on her.

Mae said in her autobiography that when she asked questions "he would either ignore me or act as if I were impossibly dumb." Yet when the white boy sitting down the row asked the exact same questions, the professor patiently explained the answers. Mae knew it was because she was an African American woman. "I gradually stopped asking questions; in fact I became too timid to ask anything. I drifted to the back row of the lecture hall," said Mae.

At a predominantly white school, being one of the only African American females in the chemical engineering major wasn't easy. Mae felt that she had to work harder than the other students to prove herself. But she was determined not to let the way she was treated get her down. Every day, she reminded herself that she was worthwhile and smart, even if others didn't see it or tell her.

"I found ways to let the wind blow around me," said Mae. "Then I opened my wings and soared on its current."

# Why Women Weren't Astronauts for a Long Time

In the 1950s and 1960s, NASA had a rule—if you wanted to be an astronaut, you first had to be a military jet test pilot. Here's the tricky part: women weren't allowed into the air force pilot training schools. With no way to become a military test pilot, there was no way a woman could ever become an astronaut.

In the late 1970s, when NASA added scientists and doctors to the new space shuttle crews, they got rid of the requirement, finally opening the door for women.

Mae began to explore other subjects in addition to science. She took African American studies and learned to speak Swahili. Unlike many of her science and engineering professors, these professors encouraged her and celebrated her intelligence. They were interested in her ideas. She realized it was important to have some professors who believed in her to balance out all those who pushed her away.

Throughout college, Mae continued to dance. She even choreographed a music and dance production. In addition to Swahili, she learned how to speak Russian and Japanese. She was elected the first female president of the Black Student Union. She graduated in 1977 with a double major:

chemical engineering and African American studies. Once college was over, Mae had to decide what to do next.

That's when a friend told her the big news. NASA had changed its policy about women in space. They were looking for female *and* minority astronauts for their new space shuttle program. They even had Nichelle Nichols—the actress who played Lieutenant Uhura on *Star Trek*—travel across the country to help recruit this new class of astronauts.

The friend thought Mae should apply.

*Should I do it?* wondered Mae.

# The Mercury 13 Should Have Been the First Women in Space

Think about the size of the first spaceships. Now think about the size of most women compared with men. Most women are lighter and smaller, breathe less oxygen, and eat less food. When space and weight are an issue—like they are in a spaceship—doesn't a woman astronaut seem like a good idea?

In 1960, the doctor in charge of the medical and mental tests for NASA's first, all-male astronauts wondered the same thing. He was curious how women would do on the tests he was giving the men. He tested a group of female pilots at his clinic. Thirteen of nineteen women passed the tests, compared to eighteen of thirty-two men. In fact, the women on average did better than the men in isolation tests. The thirteen women—now known as the Mercury 13—went on to complete the same astronaut tests as the men. One of these tests involved injecting ten-degree-Fahrenheit water into their ears!

Then NASA refused to continue the testing for women. The women took their case to Congress, calling out discrimination. Astronaut John Glenn said NASA needed to focus on the moon landing, and women in the program would complicate this goal. NASA pointed out the requirement of jet flying experience and banned the women from becoming astronauts. None of the Mercury 13 women ever went to space.

## CHAPTER 4

# Doctor Time

Mae was extremely curious and passionate about many things. She decided that, even though she'd love to be an astronaut one day, she wanted to go to medical school now. Mae didn't want to be a doctor who treated patients, though. She wanted to do biomedical engineering. Biomedical engineers are scientists who create artificial limbs and organs. She enrolled in Cornell University Medical College, in New York City. She was one of only four African American women in a class of 105 students.

Her first class was Anatomy. During the class, the students were divided into groups and each group was given a cadaver, which is a dead body.

Dissecting, or cutting open, the cadaver is one way medical students learn how human bodies work.

Seriously? Mae was panicking. She wasn't ready for this! It was only her first day!

Mae hid behind the others in her group. There was no way she was making the first incision. She felt dizzy watching the others cut. When they revealed the cadaver's insides, Mae looked away, then found herself peeking. The yellow layer of fat below the skin was kind of cool. And so were the stringy muscles. It took Mae two weeks to get totally comfortable in the lab. But soon she was standing in the front and dissecting the cadaver herself.

Homework and tests were intense in medical school, even for the best students. For much-needed study breaks, Mae took modern dance classes at the Alvin Ailey American Dance Theater. The more she danced, the more she wondered if maybe she should try to be a professional dancer instead. She called

her mother. What did she think Mae should do? Her mother said, "You can always dance if you're a doctor, but you can't doctor if you're a dancer."

Mae agreed. She graduated from medical school in 1981, then did her residency in Los Angeles. Meanwhile, in 1983, Sally Ride became the first American woman to go into space. Mae still wasn't ready to go to the stars. First, she wanted to use her new medical training.

During summer breaks in medical school, Mae had traveled to Cuba, Thailand, and Kenya.

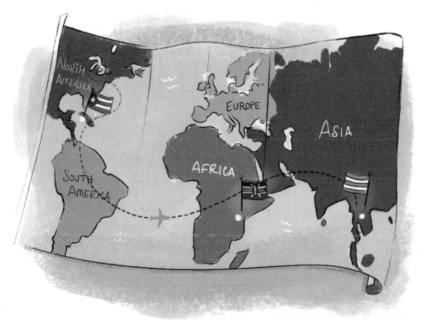

# Dr. Sally Ride: A Brief Bio

Sally Kristen Ride (1951–2012) was born in Encino, California. Just like Mae, little Sally dreamed of going into space. She loved science and math, and she was athletic. Sally was an amazing tennis player. By her junior year in high school, she was ranked eighteenth nationally on the girls' junior circuit! She thought about becoming a professional tennis player but decided to finish college instead.

Like Mae, Sally went to Stanford University, in California. She graduated with degrees in physics and English. Then she earned a master's and a PhD in physics and did research in astrophysics. In 1977, Sally saw an ad in the newspaper. For the first time ever, NASA was taking women for the astronaut training program! Sally sent in an application. So did eight thousand other people! NASA took only thirty-five people—and Sally was one of them.

For her first few assignments, Sally didn't get to go up into space. She was the capsule communicator on the ground control team and worked on the space shuttle's robotic arm. The arm was used to launch satellites. Finally, she was chosen to be a mission specialist on the space shuttle *Challenger*. On June 18, 1983, Dr. Sally Ride became the first American woman in space. The flight lasted 147 hours. Sally said it was the most fun she'd ever had. Her second flight to space in 1984 lasted 197 hours.

After NASA, Sally worked at Stanford University and at the California Space Institute, and started her own company called Sally Ride Science. She died on July 23, 2012, from pancreatic cancer.

She volunteered in remote villages and clinics that didn't have advanced health care. Mae wanted to spend more time helping people in poor areas of the world before she did graduate work in biomedical engineering. So Mae joined the Peace Corps. The Peace Corps is a US organization that promotes world peace and helps developing countries with medical care, education, and supplies. Instead of sending money, the Peace Corps sends thousands of

volunteers around the world to teach people how to improve their communities. The Peace Corps believes in the old proverb "Give a man a fish, feed him for a day; teach a man to fish, feed him for a lifetime."

Mae was assigned to be a doctor in Sierra Leone and Liberia, two countries in West Africa. She worked there from 1983 until 1985. She often had to treat patients without proper supplies or medication. Sometimes there was no electricity. She never had time off. Mae said it was the hardest job she ever had.

Mae was in charge of the medical care for thousands of Peace Corps volunteers. She was twenty-six

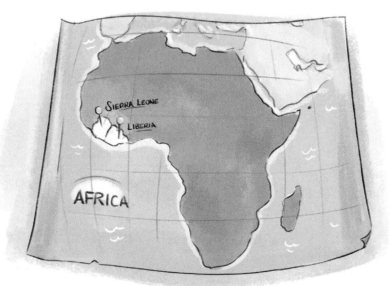

years old and had only been on the job for two weeks when one volunteer became very sick. Other doctors thought he had malaria, an infection caused by a parasite and spread by mosquito bites. Mae tried many different medicines, but nothing helped. Mae suspected the man didn't have malaria but meningitis, a disease that affects membranes around your brain and spinal cord and can be deadly. He was growing sicker and sicker—and then the hospital lost power. What now? Mae called the US Embassy and told them to send an emergency medical airplane to

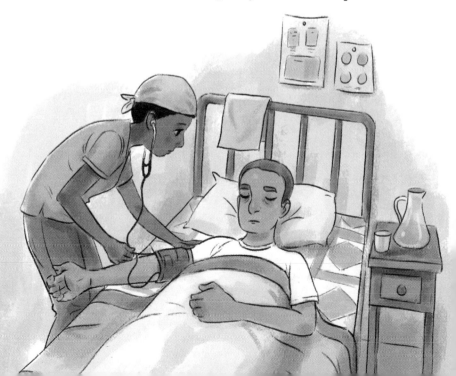

fly him to an air force hospital in Germany.

No way, said the embassy officials. The plane would cost more than $80,000 to send. They thought Mae was too inexperienced to make this big decision. Did she really know for sure that he had meningitis?

Mae couldn't prove it, but she wouldn't back down. She insisted they send the airplane right away. If not, she was afraid the man would die. They finally agreed. Mae stayed by the man's side, taking care of him, for fifty-six hours until he reached the German hospital.

It turned out Mae was right. He *did* have meningitis. She had saved his life!

"You have to learn how to do your job and you take responsibility for what you're supposed to do," Mae said later. "You can't let other people push you around."

# A Full Face of Makeup?!

When they first employed female astronauts, the men running NASA designed a special makeup kit to take into space. They assumed all women needed to wear a full face of makeup (eyeliner, mascara, eye shadow, and blush) every day while working in the space shuttle! Many men had trouble seeing Sally Ride as an "astronaut" and not a "woman astronaut."

As she was finishing up her time in the Peace Corps, one of her friends from Stanford called her. He now worked as a mechanical engineer for NASA.

"Guess what?" he said. "NASA is looking for a new batch of astronauts."

Once again, Mae had a choice to make. Astronaut or biomedical engineer? Which should she choose?

In October 1985, Mae called up NASA. *Here goes nothing,* she thought. She was sure they'd laugh at her when she asked for an application.

They didn't laugh. They sent her an application. Mae filled it out and put it in the mail. Then she returned to Los Angeles to work as a doctor. She took an extra engineering course at night. This way she'd be ready to go to graduate school if NASA didn't choose her.

She waited and waited for months for an answer.

## CHAPTER 5

# Getting In

Tragedy struck before NASA told Mae their decision. On January 28, 1986, the space shuttle *Challenger* exploded only seventy-three seconds after lift-off. All seven astronauts on board—including high school teacher Christa McAuliffe—died. The accident shocked the world. NASA stopped all shuttle missions until they could figure out what went wrong. They also stopped looking for new astronauts. Mae's application—and thousands of others—went into a file drawer.

NASA's scientists finally discovered that a part on the rocket booster had failed, because the air temperature had been so cold the morning of the launch. Many people found it scary that one tiny part could cause such destruction and death. They wondered if space travel should continue. NASA thought it should. A year later, NASA started hiring new astronauts again. Did Mae still want to apply for such a dangerous job?

Yes! She sent in an updated application. A few weeks later, her telephone rang. It was NASA. Could she come to the Johnson Space Center, in Houston, next week for an interview?

Um . . . of course!

What did Mae do next? She raced to a book-store and bought all the books she could find on the history of space exploration. Then she worried about her hair. She'd just gotten it cut in a short Afro. Would NASA think she was too edgy—especially for a Black woman—to be an astronaut?

# The First Black Astronauts

**Robert Henry Lawrence Jr.** (1935–1967) was the first African American astronaut in a national space program. Born in Chicago, he had a PhD in physical chemistry and was an ace test and fighter pilot. In 1967, he was chosen for the Air Force's Manned Orbiting Laboratory (MOL) program, which was sort of a spy-in-the-sky program. A few months later, Robert sat in the back seat of an F-104 *Starfighter* jet, teaching another pilot a new landing technique that would later be used in the space shuttle program. Their jet crashed and, while the pilot's seat ejected right away, Robert's seat didn't eject until the plane had rolled onto its side and was on fire. Robert died before ever getting the chance to go to space. (When MOL shut down in 1969, many of their astronauts were transferred to NASA.)

**Guion "Guy" Stewart Bluford Jr.** (1942– ) is the first African American astronaut to fly to space. Before joining NASA in 1978, he received a PhD in aerospace engineering and was a US Air Force pilot in the Vietnam War. Guy made history when he soared into space as a mission specialist on August 30, 1983, on the *Challenger* space shuttle. He flew four shuttle missions and spent 688 hours in space before retiring in 1993.

Mae couldn't do anything about it now. She'd just go and be herself.

In Houston, Mae had to undergo every kind of medical test imaginable. There were eye exams and hearing tests. They had her run on a treadmill. They listened to her heartbeat. They checked her muscle strength. They took her blood. They made sure that nothing was out of the ordinary.

Then they gave her a claustrophobia test. Claustrophobia is a fear of enclosed or small spaces. Why did they test this? Astronauts are often in tight, cramped spaces for long periods of time. NASA didn't want anyone having a panic attack during a mission.

Mae was instructed to sit inside a beach ball that was only three feet in diameter. She had to sit calmly, knees to chin, for thirty minutes in complete darkness. Air blew inside so she could breathe, but she couldn't move. She was wired to a pulse monitor, so NASA could track her body's response.

Mae squeezed inside the ball. She had no clock and everyone left the room. Did Mae freak out? Far from it! She began to sing—and then she fell asleep!

Next, Mae was given other psychological exams and watched to see how she worked in a group. She was also interviewed by the FBI, the Federal Bureau of Investigation. The FBI interviewed her family and friends, too. They wanted to make sure she'd never

committed a crime and was a good citizen. Mae had nothing to hide.

Mae went back to Los Angeles and took care of her patients. Months and months of waiting went by. Finally, one day in June 1987, her office phone rang. It was NASA.

"Would you still like to be an astronaut?" the man on the phone asked.

"Yes. Absolutely!" cried Mae.

"Welcome on board," he said. Then he told her that she couldn't tell anyone until NASA made their official announcement the following day.

No one? Not her parents? Not her sister?

Mae wasn't sure she could keep such a big secret. That night, she took two cardio-funk dance classes to stay busy. But when she got back to her apartment, she couldn't hold in her excitement.

She was one of fifteen astronauts chosen out of the two thousand who'd applied!

She was the first African American woman!

In fact, she was the first woman of color anywhere in the world to be chosen to be an astronaut!

This was amazing!

She just had to tell someone . . .

She turned to Sneeze, her cat. "We're moving to Houston!" she cried.

Sneeze was completely cool with it.

## CHAPTER 6

# Facing Her Fears

Mae wasn't an astronaut just yet. First, she would have to complete the tough astronaut training program at the Johnson Space Center.

Her classmates came from all over the country and from all different backgrounds. Some had been test pilots, while others were meteorologists, astrophysicists, or mechanical engineers. Now they all had to learn the same things. They spent a lot of time in the classroom. They studied astronomy, meteorology, physics, and rocket propulsion. They learned how the space shuttle worked and how to fix every part, in case something broke or went wrong.

They trained in the mission simulator. The mission simulator is a full-size model of the space shuttle that never leaves the ground. Even though Mae wouldn't be a pilot, she still had to learn what every switch, lever, and warning light meant. She had to learn how to fly and navigate.

When Mae and her classmates weren't sitting at their desks or in the simulator, they exercised. Astronauts must be in excellent physical shape to wear the heavy space suit. The space suit weighs

about three hundred pounds. That's like carrying a gorilla on your back!

The astronaut candidates learned how to pilot many kinds of aircraft. They learned to scuba dive. They were ejected from a high-flying plane to experience how the ejector seat worked. Their open parachute was tied to the back of a motorboat and they were dragged through the cold ocean so they could learn to untangle themselves from the parachute's harness without drowning.

They had survival training in the woods and in the ocean. In an emergency landing, an astronaut could end up anywhere. In the ocean, they had to swim long distances and tread water. In the wilderness,  they had to build shelters and find food. They had to use a compass to navigate their way to safety. They learned to build a fire with flint and weave fishing nets from the cords on their parachutes.

Every astronaut was challenged. One time, Mae was handed a dead bird to clean and prepare to eat. "They decided they wanted to pick on me . . . I'm probably the worst person to pick on," she said. "I used to hunt with my dad. I'm a doctor. You can't gross me out. I've worked in Africa. I've worked with all kinds of diseases."

Mae plucked the bird's feathers and scooped out its insides without flinching. Survival training didn't scare Mae. But learning to parachute and being dropped into the ocean from a helicopter to prac-tice water rescues did.

Since she was a lit-tle girl, she'd been frightened of heights. When it was her turn, Mae stood in the open doorway of the whirring helicopter. Her knees trembled. She was afraid to look down. They wanted her to jump? For real?

*What if I can't finish the training because I'm too scared?* she worried.

"There was no way I was not going to get through because of my fear of heights," Mae once told a

journalist. She took a deep breath, embraced her fear, and . . . jumped. From then on, Mae made a point of working on her weaknesses. "I do things with my left hand just to see if I can."

NASA trained the astronauts to deal with weightlessness. In outer space, there is only a small amount of gravity, or microgravity. Gravity is an invisible force that holds us down. When you jump up, gravity brings your body back to the ground. Without gravity, human bodies—and other objects—float.

The feeling you get floating in water is similar to the weightlessness of space, so Mae wore her bulky space suit in a giant indoor pool. For six-hour stretches underwater, she practiced space walks and doing tasks in the space shuttle. She trained her body to adjust to microgravity. It was exhausting!

Then there was the "Vomit Comet."

That's the nickname for a special airplane that's basically a high-flying roller coaster. The plane flies in arcs, making huge dips and plunges. While the

plane is in free fall, astronauts experience weightlessness for about twenty seconds before the plane
pulls up out of the dive. One out of every three pas-
sengers barfs. Each flight lasts about two to three
hours and makes about fifty dives. And each trainee
is expected to ride the Vomit Comet hundreds of
times! That's a lot of vomit!

Mae passed all the tests—even the Vomit Comet. She completed her yearlong training and got her official astronaut pin. Mae was ready to blast off into space!

Not so fast . . .

Mae had to wait her turn. Missions didn't go up very often. Some astronauts had been waiting for over five years to go into space. Some never ever got the chance to go.

Mae added her name to a long list. She looked at all the names ahead of hers and sighed. She was the only African American woman on the list.

Since putting a man on the moon, it had taken NASA more than twenty years to open their doors to minority women. Mae had worked hard, but prejudice and racism still existed.

Would she ever be sent on a mission up to the stars?

National Aeronautics and Space Administration

Group 12

Curtis L. Brown Jr
Nancy Jan Davis
Robert L. Gibson
Michael R. Clifford
Jay Apt
Mark C. Lee
Bruce E. Melnick
Mamoru Mohri
Gregory J. Harbaugh
Mae C. Jemison

# QUIZ:
# Do You Have What It Takes to Be an Astronaut?

Answer these questions to see if you're ready to blast off.

What do you want to study in college?

**A.** Cooking

**B.** Writing

**C.** Science and math

How often do you exercise or play sports?

**A.** Never

**B.** Once a week

**C.** 3–4 times a week

How do you feel about roller coasters?

**A.** Hate them.

**B.** Like them but sometimes get queasy.

**C.** Love them. The more steep drops the better!

You're riding your bike and it breaks down. You:

**A.** Ditch it and walk home.

**B.** Call your parents and help them bring it to the repair shop.

**C.** Inspect the gears, pedals, and tires to see what went wrong and if you can fix it.

Could you be away from your friends and family for six months?

**A.** Never

**B.** Maybe

**C.** Sure

You need to do a group project in class. How well do you work with others?

**A.** Horribly. I prefer to go solo.

**B.** Okay. I can make it work.

**C.** Great. Teamwork is my middle name.

You have a test tomorrow, you have to babysit your cranky little brother, your computer breaks, and your dog starts to vomit (all at the same time) . . . how are you feeling?

**A.** Totally stressed out. You curl up and whimper.

**B.** Somewhat stressed. You yell at the dog, but you still hold it together.

**C.** Chill. You take deep breaths and stay zen.

How long can you hold your breath?

**A.** 10 seconds

**B.** 30 seconds

**C.** 60 seconds

In this pattern, what comes next? O OO OOO

**A.** O

**B.** OOO

**C.** OOOO

How did you do? Add up how many times you chose C for your answer.

**0–4:** Astronaut training may not be your thing—but there are plenty of aerospace jobs that let you keep your feet on the ground and your eyes to the sky.

**5–7:** You're almost there . . . just need a bit more training.

**8–9:** Get out your space suit! You're ready for the next mission!

## CHAPTER 7

# Lift-off!

While she waited, Mae worked in NASA's offices and labs. She was given Sally Ride's old desk. In 1989, Mae was finally chosen to go into space. She was assigned to fly on the space shuttle *Endeavour* as a science mission specialist. She'd perform science experiments in space. *Endeavour* wouldn't launch for several years, so Mae and the other scientists were sent to Japan to get their experiments ready.

*Endeavour* STS-47 would be a historic mission for many reasons. It was the fiftieth space shuttle mission. It was the first joint mission between the United States and Japan. The first married astronaut couple were on board. And Mae would be the first African American woman in space.

# Married Astronauts?

Once NASA started sending female astronauts to space, they made a rule that married couples could not be launched together. They felt a married couple on board would change how the crew acted with one another. Mark Lee and Jan Davis were chosen to be astronauts on *Endeavour*. They first met during training and secretly got married a few weeks before launch. What did NASA do when they found out? Since they couldn't cancel the mission and there wasn't enough time to train a new crew member, NASA broke their own rule and let them fly together.

On the morning of September 12, 1992, Mae and the six other members of the *Endeavour* crew were fitted into their orange flight suits. Every strap was checked and tightened. Earphones and communications systems were tested. Then they rode a bus to the launchpad at the Kennedy Space Center, in Florida. The enormous space shuttle with its huge external fuel tank and two rocket boosters rose thirty stories high. Mae and the other astronauts took an elevator to the crew waiting area on top of a 374-foot-high scaffold.

A final check of the shuttle was performed. Then it was time to climb inside. Lying on her back with her feet above her head, Mae buckled into seat number six. The hatch snapped shut. And the countdown began.

5 . . . 4 . . .

The main engines ignited with a *whoosh!*

3 . . . 2 . . . 1 . . .

Lift-off!

On the ground, Mae's mother cried, "My baby's on top of an inferno!"

The powerful rocket boosters blasted the shuttle upward. Higher and higher. The shuttle rattled and shook violently. Mae's spine tingled. Crushing pressure pushed against her chest. Her body felt three times heavier as they shot through the atmosphere. The shuttle accelerated twenty-five times faster than an average race car.

*Boom!* Two minutes later, the rocket boosters separated from the shuttle and parachuted into the ocean. The external fuel tank now provided the shuttle with speed and power.

# Space Shuttle Fast Facts

✧ The space shuttle was the first spacecraft that could carry humans and be used again.

✧ It took off like a rocket but landed on a runway like an airplane.

- Five space shuttles made a total of 135 space flights, carrying astronauts and cargo.

- The first shuttle flight was in 1981 and the last shuttle flight was in 2011.

- The white part of the shuttle is called the orbiter. It is the only part that orbits Earth.

- The shuttle traveled around Earth at a speed of about 17,500 miles (28,000 kilometers) per hour. The crew saw a sunrise or sunset every forty-five minutes!

On the ground, Mae's mother hugged her father. The dangerous lift-off had been a success!

Eight minutes into the flight, the fuel tank fell away. *Endeavour* began its first orbit around Earth. All grew quiet inside the shuttle. Mae took a deep breath, then got busy. She gathered the astronauts' orange launch-and-entry suits and stowed them.

"Mae, come up to the flight deck." The shuttle commander's voice crackled over her headset.

Wearing only her thermal underwear from launch, Mae floated through the opening from mid-deck to the flight deck. What was going on?

"Look." The commander pointed. "Chicago is coming up."

Mae peered out the window for the first time. The city of Chicago came into view far, far below. Mae smiled when she saw her hometown. Not so long ago, she was a little girl standing down there looking up. And now she was up here.

In outer space.

Among the stars.

It was magical.

## CHAPTER 8

# Busy in Space

Mae wasn't on board to sightsee. She quickly returned to the cargo area. There were over forty experiments to complete. It was time to get the lab up and running.

The crew's experiments were done in Spacelab-J. The lab was a cylinder-like capsule the size of a small bus. It was in the cargo bay. An eight-foot tunnel connected it to the crew's quarters. The crew was divided into red and blue teams. One team would work while the other slept so scientists could do the experiments around the clock. Mae was on the blue team. She often worked twelve hours at a time.

Mae's experiments all had to do with

weightlessness. She tested to see if frog eggs could develop into tadpoles in zero gravity. They did. And when the tadpoles were returned to Earth, they turned into healthy frogs.

Then she tested how weightlessness affects humans.

Zero gravity can be tons of fun. You can sleep standing up. You can eat upside down. But people get spacesick, too. In zero gravity, the fluids in your body move into your head. Your face gets puffy. Your nose gets congested. You feel tired and queasy. Your eyeballs even flatten out! Most astronauts get spacesick, especially on their first few days in orbit. There is medicine to take, but it makes an astronaut very sleepy. NASA wanted to find natural ways to help the crew.

Mae experimented on herself and other crew members to see if biofeedback could help. Biofeedback is a calming technique where people use their minds to control their body's functions. It's similar to the power of positive thinking.

Mae strapped monitors to her body. She tracked all her vital signs, such as temperature, breathing, blood pressure, and heart rate. When she started to feel motion sick, she'd see what vital sign was affected. Then she'd try to relax that part of her body and mentally control her breathing or sweating. Doctors and scientists back on Earth reviewed her data. They liked the results. NASA continues to use and experiment with biofeedback today.

Mae was in space for eight days—or 190 hours, 30 minutes, and 23 seconds. She made 126 orbits around the Earth. Mae started every day by saying, "Hailing frequencies open." This famous greeting came from *Star Trek*, the TV show that first made her believe a girl like her could someday go into space.

Each astronaut on board was allowed to bring a few small personal items with them. Mae took:

- a statuette from West Africa to symbolize that space belongs to all nations

- a photo of Bessie Coleman, the first African American woman to get a pilot's license

- a Chicago Bulls jersey from basketball player Michael Jordan to remind her of her hometown

- an Alvin Ailey American Dance Theater poster, because "science and dance are both expressions of the boundless creativity that people have to share with one another."

# My Space Packing List

If you were traveling to space, what three special things would you bring?

1. _____

2. _____

3. _____

Mae found dancing with no gravity tricky, but she said, "the incredible thing about being in space is you can keep spinning and spinning!"

As the crew prepared to return to Earth, Mae took long looks out the shuttle window. "I felt like I belonged right there in space," she wrote in her autobiography. "I realized I would feel comfortable anywhere in the universe—because I belonged to and was a part of it, as much as any star, planet, asteroid, comet, or nebula."

*Endeavour* landed at Kennedy Space Center in Florida on September 20, 1992.

When she got home, the city of Chicago threw a six-day celebration in her honor. Mae Jemison was famous! She had changed the face of space exploration.

Now that she'd gone to the stars, what was next? Should she write her name on the list to go on another mission?

Or should she use her fame to help other people?

## CHAPTER 9

# Next Chapters

Six months after her shuttle flight, Mae decided to leave NASA. A lot of people told her she was making a big mistake. They wanted her to go into space again. But Mae said being an astronaut was only one part of her life.

"I had other things that I needed to contribute. What difference does it make if I was the first woman of color to go into space if I didn't use my position to make other things happen? We have . . . to move the world forward," she said in a *Newsweek* magazine interview.

In her resignation letter to NASA, Mae explained that she planned to focus on "teaching, mentoring, health care issues, and increasing participation in science and technology of those who have traditionally been left out."

She took a job as a professor at Dartmouth College and taught a course called "Space Age Technology in Developing Countries." Then she started her own company, the Jemison Group, in Houston, Texas. The company's mission is to help people become involved in space exploration, promote science education, and use technology to make life better in countries with less money and less industry. For example, they've brought solar power and satellite-based communication systems to West African countries.

Mae wants to get kids, especially girls and young people of color, as excited about science as she is. She started The Earth We Share, an international science camp for students ages twelve to sixteen.

Mae also founded the 100 Year Starship project. Its goal is to get humans ready to travel beyond our solar system within the next hundred years. "We still have to figure out how to feed ourselves and

maintain equipment," Mae has pointed out. "All the things that we need to do a successful interstellar mission are the things that we need to live successfully here on Earth . . . energy . . . recycling . . . how we interact with one another." A journey beyond our solar system would take many years. Mae is tackling the big questions beyond the mechanics of getting there: How do you have enough clothes and

medicine? What do you do with your trash? How do you grow food? How do you care for the old and the sick?

Mae encourages people of all ages and backgrounds to come up with bold new scientific ideas. New technologies created for future interstellar space travel can make life better on Earth today. Did you know that cell phones, ATMs, and GPS all started as space technology experiments?

# What Is Interstellar Travel?

Interstellar travel is travel beyond our solar system to other stars or galaxies. The universe is made up of galaxies. A galaxy is a huge group of planets, stars, dust, and gas. Earth is in the Milky Way galaxy. Our solar system—the sun and the eight planets (Mercury, Venus, Earth, Mars, Jupiter, Saturn, Uranus, Neptune) that orbit it plus their many moons—is all part of the Milky Way. The closest known star system to our sun is Alpha Centauri. It is *trillions* of miles away from Earth. With the technology we have now, it would take a starship tens of thousands of years to reach Alpha Centauri. Scientists are working on how to travel there much faster. An interstellar journey for humans may seem impossible now, but what if you think about it like this? The first airplane flight was in 1903, and the first human landed on the moon in 1969, just sixty-six years later. Can you imagine where our space program will be by the time you're sixty-six years old?

Throughout her life, Mae has received honors and awards from important organizations. Can you guess two of her favorite honors? She was asked to be an actress on an episode of her favorite TV show, *Star Trek: The Next Generation*, and LEGO made a Mae Jemison astronaut figurine!

Would Mae ever be an astronaut again? "I'd love to go into space again if there were a mission to Mars," said Mae. "I'd also love to go to a completely different planetary system, out of our solar system."

Mae was never afraid to dream big. As a little girl, she set her sights on the stars. She refused to accept that she didn't belong or couldn't do something because of her gender or her skin color. She fought her fears and used inner strength to make a place for herself, even when there wasn't one or others weren't welcoming. Mae became a great astronaut—and also a great doctor, scientist, dancer, businesswoman, and teacher.

"I still look up at the stars and it gives me hope, and it gives me energy," said Mae. "I think one of the things that we have to think about is, we are all a part of this universe."

# Six Quotes by Mae

Mae's life and attitude are an inspiration. Here are six amazing things she's said . . .

1.  "Even though folks might doubt me, I didn't doubt myself."

2.  "Never be limited by other people's limited imaginations . . . If you adopt their attitudes, then the possibility won't exist because you'll have already shut it out."

3.  "People can put obstacles in front of you, and you have a choice. You can sit there and try to make them change or you can go around it."

4. "I like to think of ideas as potential energy. They're really wonderful, but nothing will happen until we risk putting them into action."

5. "People don't see women—particularly Black women—in science and technology fields. My participation in the space shuttle mission helps to say that all peoples of the world have astronomers, physicists, and explorers."

6. "Some of the most fun people I know are scientists."

# Timeline:
# Dr. Mae Jemison

**1956**
Born on October 17 in Decatur, Alabama

**1959**
Moves to Chicago, Illinois

**1973**
Graduates from Morgan Park High School at age 16

**1985**
Applies to be an astronaut at NASA

**1987**
Is selected as an astronaut candidate

## 1977
Graduates from
Stanford University

## 1981
Graduates from
Cornell University
Medical College

## 1983
Volunteers as a
medical officer with
the Peace Corps in
Sierra Leone and
Liberia, West Africa

## 1992
Becomes the first female
African American astronaut
to go into space. Works as a
mission specialist aboard the
space shuttle *Endeavour*.

## 1993
Retires from NASA.
Starts the Jemison
Group.

# Timeline:
# Women in Spaceflight

**1958**
United States
government forms
NASA

**1962**
Thirteen women pass
NASA's physical tests,
yet none are selected
for the program

**1963**
Russian cosmonaut
Valentina Tereshkova
becomes the first
woman in space

**1992**
Mae Jemison is the
first African American
woman in space

**1993**
Ellen Ochoa becomes
the first Hispanic
woman in space

**1995**
Eileen Collins becomes
the first woman to
pilot a space shuttle

**2002**
Peggy Whitson
becomes the first
female scientist
to work at the
International Space
Station

**2006**
Anousheh
Ansari becomes the
first Muslim woman
in space

**2007**
Sunita Williams
becomes the first
astronaut to run a
marathon in space (on
a treadmill)

## 1982
Russian cosmonaut Svetlana Savitskaya becomes the second woman in space

## 1983
Sally Ride becomes the first American woman in space

## 1984
Svetlana Savitskaya becomes the first woman to walk in space. Kathryn Sullivan is the first American to walk in space later this year

## 1997
Kalpana Chawla becomes the first Indian American woman in space

## 1999
Eileen Collins becomes the first female commander of a space shuttle mission

## 2008
Peggy Whitson becomes the first woman to command the International Space Station

## 2017
Peggy Whitson completes the most total time in space (665 days cumulative) by any American astronaut, male or female

# VIP Hall of Fame

Mae Jemison was a trailblazer for women in STEM. Here are a few other African American women who have led the way in science, technology, engineering, and math:

**Ashanti Johnson** was the first African American female chemical oceanographer. She analyzes how past big environmental events (like oil spills) have impacted our coasts and our lives.

**Joycelyn Elders** worked as a pediatrician and public health administrator before she became the first African American Surgeon General of the United States.

**Aprille Ericsson** is one of the most famous women at NASA today. She's worked on spacecrafts and instruments that help us understand space science and the Earth.

**Lisette Titre-Montgomery** used her knowledge of computer programming to become one of America's leading video game artists and designers. She's worked on games like "Tiger Woods Golf," "The Simpsons," and "South Park."

# Bibliography

Alagna, Magdalena. *Mae Jemison*. New York: Rosen Publishing Group, 2004.

Calkhoven, Laurie. *You Should Meet Mae Jemison*. New York: Simon Spotlight, 2016.

Jemison, Mae. *Find Where the Wind Goes: Moments from My Life*. New York: Scholastic, 2001.

Yannuzzi, Della A. *Mae Jemison: A Space Biography*. New Jersey: Enslow Publishers, 1998.

# Further Reading

*Women in Space: 23 Stories of First Flights, Scientific Missions and Gravity-Breaking Adventures* by Karen Bush Gibson

*Reaching for the Moon* by Buzz Aldrin, illustrated by Wendell Minor

*Hidden Figures Young Readers' Edition* by Margot Lee Shetterly

*13 Planets: The Latest View of the Solar System* by David A. Aguilar

*Apollo 13 (Totally True Adventures): How Three Brave Astronauts Survived a Space Disaster* by Kathleen Weidner Zoehfeld, illustrated by Wesley Lowe

*Exploring Constellations* by Sara L. Latta

*Exploring Space: From Galileo to the Mars Rover and Beyond* by Martin Jenkins, illustrated by Stephen Biesty

# About the Author

Heather Alexander is the author of many nonfiction and fiction books for kids. She lives in Los Angeles, California, and tries to look up at the stars every night (although they're not always easy to see in the city!). Visit her at www.heatheralexanderbooks.com.